RESPIRATORY DISEASES AND DISORDERS

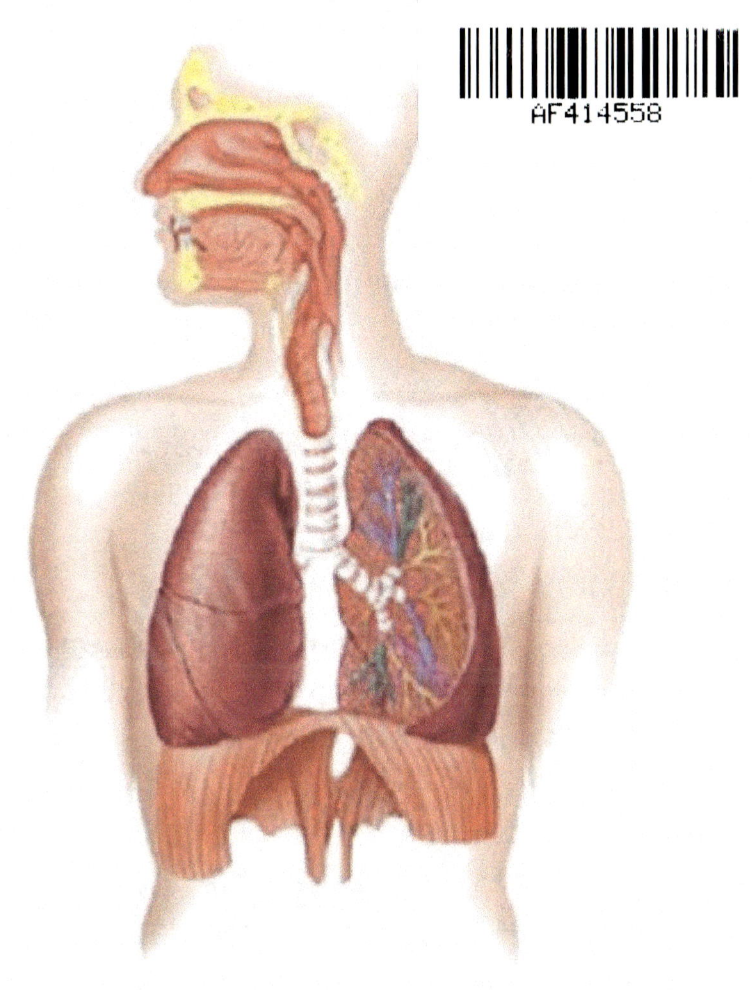

TABLE OF CONTENTS

<u>**COURSE OVERVIEW**</u>

This course provides an in-depth exploration of respiratory diseases and disorders, tailored for healthcare providers who seek to enhance their understanding and management of these conditions. Covering a wide range of topics from common respiratory conditions such as asthma, COPD, pneumonia, and lung cancer to specialized areas like occupational respiratory diseases and pulmonary hypertension, the course offers a thorough grounding in the pathophysiology, diagnosis, treatment, and management strategies of each condition.

<u>**COURSE OBJECTIVE**</u>

By the end of this course, participants will be able to describe the underlying pathophysiological mechanisms of major respiratory diseases, including asthma, COPD, pneumonia, and lung cancer. They will also recognize the risk factors, causes, and epidemiological trends of various respiratory disorders. Finally, they will be able to utilize diagnostic tools and techniques effectively to identify and differentiate between various respiratory conditions.

This course aims to provide healthcare providers with a robust foundation in respiratory medicine, ensuring they are well-prepared to meet the demands of clinical practice and improve patient care outcomes.

<u>**COURSE MATERIALS**</u>

To learn this course, **healthcare providers/ participants** must be provided with materials like a Pen, pencil, notebook, and notepad to better understand and make it easy for them to learn.

INTRODUCTION

Respiratory diseases and disorders encompass a wide range of conditions that affect the lungs and airways. These conditions vary in severity from mild, self-limiting illnesses to severe, life-threatening diseases. Understanding the intricacies of respiratory diseases is crucial for healthcare providers to provide effective care and improve patient outcomes.

Respiratory diseases are a significant global health burden, contributing to substantial morbidity and mortality rates. They affect millions of people worldwide, with conditions such as asthma, chronic obstructive pulmonary disease (COPD), pneumonia, and lung cancer being among the most prevalent. These diseases not only impact the quality of life of individuals but also pose a significant economic burden on healthcare systems due to direct medical costs and loss of productivity.

This course is designed to equip healthcare providers with comprehensive knowledge about various respiratory diseases and disorders. It aims to provide insights into the causes, symptoms, diagnostic techniques, treatment options, and management strategies for these conditions. By enhancing their understanding of respiratory diseases, healthcare providers can improve their diagnostic accuracy, treatment efficacy, and overall patient care.

MODULE ONE

LESSON ONE: RESPIRATORY DISEASES AND DISORDERS

Respiratory diseases and disorders represent a broad spectrum of conditions affecting the respiratory system, including the airways, lungs, and respiratory muscles. These conditions can be

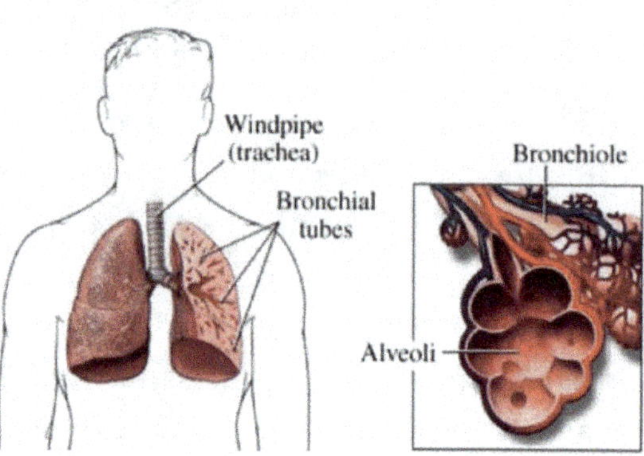

classified into obstructive, restrictive, infectious, and neoplastic categories, each with distinct pathophysiological mechanisms, clinical presentations, and management strategies.

One of the fundamental aspects of respiratory diseases is understanding their etiology. Respiratory conditions can arise from various factors, including genetic predisposition, environmental exposures, infections, and lifestyle choices. For instance, smoking is a well-known risk factor for many respiratory diseases, particularly COPD and lung cancer. Environmental pollutants and occupational hazards also play a significant role in the development and exacerbation of respiratory conditions.

Another critical component is recognizing the symptoms associated with respiratory diseases. These symptoms can vary widely depending on the specific condition but often include coughing, shortness of breath, wheezing, chest pain, and fatigue. Early recognition of these symptoms is essential for timely diagnosis and intervention, which can significantly improve patient outcomes.

Diagnostic techniques in respiratory medicine have advanced significantly over the years. From basic tools such as chest X-rays and spirometry to more sophisticated methods like computed tomography (CT) scans and bronchoscopy, these techniques help in accurately diagnosing and assessing the severity of respiratory conditions. Understanding the appropriate use and interpretation of these diagnostic tools is crucial for healthcare providers.

Treatment and management of respiratory diseases require a multifaceted approach. Pharmacological treatments, including bronchodilators, corticosteroids, antibiotics, and targeted therapies, play a central role in managing these conditions. Non-pharmacological strategies such as pulmonary rehabilitation, lifestyle modifications, and patient education are also vital components of comprehensive care. Additionally, preventive measures such as vaccination and smoking cessation programs are essential in reducing the incidence and impact of respiratory diseases.

CLASSIFICATION AND EPIDEMIOLOGY

Understanding the classification of respiratory diseases is the first step in grasping their complexity. Obstructive diseases, such as asthma and COPD, are characterized by airflow limitation, while restrictive diseases, such as pulmonary fibrosis, involve reduced lung volumes. Infectious diseases, like pneumonia and tuberculosis, are caused by pathogenic microorganisms, and neoplastic diseases, such as lung cancer, involve abnormal cell growth within the lung tissues.

Respiratory diseases are a leading cause of morbidity and mortality worldwide. According to the World Health Organization (WHO), respiratory infections, COPD, and lung cancer are among the top causes of death globally. Various factors, including geographic location, socioeconomic status, lifestyle choices, and environmental exposures, influence the prevalence of these conditions.

PATHOPHYSIOLOGY

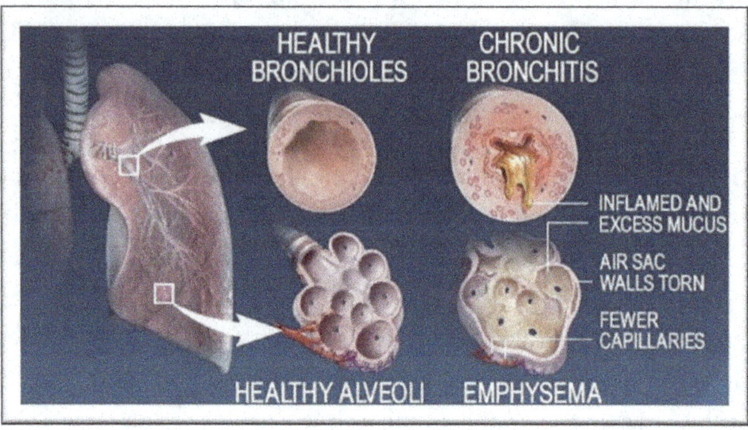

The pathophysiology of respiratory diseases varies significantly between different conditions but often involves inflammation, tissue damage, and impaired gas exchange. In obstructive diseases like asthma and COPD, chronic inflammation leads to airway narrowing and airflow limitation. In asthma, this is often reversible with treatment, while in COPD, the damage is typically irreversible and progressive.

Restrictive diseases such as pulmonary fibrosis involve scarring and stiffening of the lung tissues, leading to reduced lung compliance and difficulty in expanding the lungs. Infectious diseases like pneumonia cause inflammation and consolidation of lung tissue, impairing oxygen exchange. Lung cancer involves the uncontrolled growth of abnormal cells, which can invade and destroy normal lung tissue, causing a variety of respiratory symptoms.

RISK FACTORS

Several risk factors contribute to the development and progression of respiratory diseases. Smoking is the most significant modifiable risk factor, particularly for COPD and lung cancer. Other environmental factors, such as exposure to air pollution, occupational hazards, and allergens, also play crucial roles. Genetic predisposition can influence susceptibility to certain conditions, such as asthma and cystic fibrosis.

CLINICAL MANIFESTATIONS

Respiratory diseases present with a range of symptoms that can vary in intensity and frequency. Common symptoms include:

- **Cough:** A reflex action to clear the airways, often seen in infections, asthma, COPD, and lung cancer.
- **Dyspnea (shortness of breath)** is a subjective sensation of difficulty breathing commonly seen in almost all respiratory conditions.
- **Wheezing**: A high-pitched whistling sound during breathing, typically associated with asthma and COPD.
- **Chest pain** Can result from infections, pleural involvement, or malignancies.
- **Fatigue:** A non-specific symptom often associated with chronic respiratory diseases.

DIAGNOSTIC APPROACHES

Accurate diagnosis of respiratory diseases relies on a combination of clinical evaluation, imaging studies, and laboratory tests. Key diagnostic tools include:

- **Chest X-ray:** A fundamental imaging modality to detect abnormalities such as infections, tumors, and structural changes.
- **Spirometry:** Measures lung function and is essential for diagnosing obstructive and restrictive diseases.
- **CT Scan:** This procedure provides detailed cross-sectional images of the chest, useful for identifying complex conditions such as tumors and interstitial lung diseases.
- **Bronchoscopy:** Allows direct visualization of the airways and is useful for biopsy and removal of foreign bodies.

MANAGEMENT STRATEGIES

The management of respiratory diseases involves both pharmacological and non-pharmacological approaches. Pharmacological treatments include:

- **Bronchodilators:** Medications that relax airway muscles, used primarily in asthma and COPD.
- **Corticosteroids:** Anti-inflammatory agents used to reduce airway inflammation in asthma and other inflammatory conditions.
- **Antibiotics:** Used to treat bacterial infections such as pneumonia.
- **Targeted therapies:** Include monoclonal antibodies and tyrosine kinase inhibitors for specific conditions like lung cancer.

Non-pharmacological strategies encompass:

- **Pulmonary rehabilitation:** A comprehensive program including exercise training, education, and support for patients with chronic respiratory diseases.
- **Lifestyle modifications:** Smoking cessation, weight management, and avoidance of environmental triggers.
- **Vaccination:** Prevention of respiratory infections through immunization against pathogens like influenza and pneumococcus.

LESSON TWO: ASTHMA: UNDERSTANDING THE BASICS AND BEYOND

Asthma is a chronic inflammatory disorder of the airways characterized by variable and recurring symptoms, airflow obstruction, bronchial hyperresponsiveness, and underlying inflammation. It affects individuals of all ages and is one of the most common chronic diseases worldwide.

Asthma - Inflamed Bronchial Tube

normal

asthma

EPIDEMIOLOGY

Asthma affects an estimated 300 million people globally, with varying prevalence across different regions. It is more common in developed countries, possibly due to environmental and lifestyle factors. Although it can develop at any age, it often begins in childhood. It is a leading cause of hospitalizations and emergency room visits, particularly among children.

PATHOPHYSIOLOGY

The hallmark of asthma is chronic inflammation of the airways, which leads to airway hyperresponsiveness and obstruction. A complex interplay of genetic and environmental factors mediates this inflammation. Key inflammatory cells involved include eosinophils, T-lymphocytes, and mast cells.

TRIGGERS

Asthma symptoms can be triggered by a variety of factors, including:

- Allergens: Pollen, dust mites, pet dander, and mold.

- Infections: Respiratory viruses, particularly in children.
- Exercise: Physical activity can induce bronchoconstriction in some individuals.
- Occupational exposures: Chemicals, dust, and fumes in the workplace.
- Air pollution: Smoke, car exhaust, and industrial emissions.
- Weather changes: Cold air and sudden weather shifts.
- Medications: Some drugs, such as beta-blockers and aspirin, can exacerbate asthma symptoms.
- Food additives: Sulfites and other preservatives in foods and beverages.

CLINICAL MANIFESTATIONS

Asthma symptoms can vary widely in severity and frequency, ranging from occasional episodes to persistent and severe symptoms. Common clinical manifestations include:

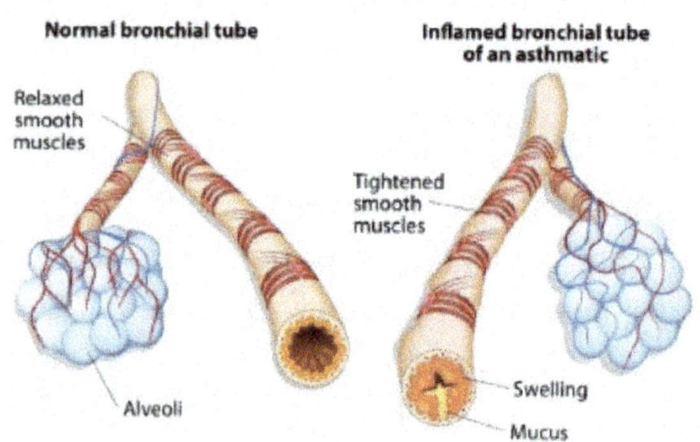

- Wheezing: A high-pitched, musical sound heard primarily during exhalation.
- Coughing: Often worse at night or early in the morning.
- Shortness of breath: A sensation of breathlessness or difficulty breathing.
- Chest tightness: A feeling of constriction or pressure in the chest.

DIAGNOSIS

Diagnosing asthma involves a combination of clinical assessment, pulmonary function tests, and sometimes additional investigations to rule out other conditions. Key diagnostic steps include:

- Medical history: Detailed inquiry about symptoms, triggers, family history, and past medical history.
- Physical examination: Listening for wheezing and assessing for signs of other conditions.
- Spirometry: Measures lung function, specifically looking at forced expiratory volume in one second (FEV1) and forced vital capacity (FVC). A significant improvement in FEV1 after bronchodilator administration supports the diagnosis of asthma.
- Peak expiratory flow (PEF) monitoring: Daily measurement can help track asthma control and variability.
- Allergy testing: Identifying specific allergens that may trigger asthma symptoms.

MANAGEMENT

Effective management of asthma requires a personalized approach that includes both pharmacological and non-pharmacological strategies.

Pharmacological Treatment

- Inhaled corticosteroids (ICS): The cornerstone of asthma treatment, reducing airway inflammation and preventing symptoms.
- Long-acting beta-agonists (LABAs): Used in combination with ICS to provide long-term bronchodilation.
- Short-acting beta-agonists (SABAs): For quick relief of acute symptoms.
- Leukotriene receptor antagonists: Alternative or add-on therapy for some patients.

- Biologic therapies: Target specific pathways in severe asthma, such as anti-IgE or anti-IL-5 antibodies.

Non-Pharmacological Strategies

- **Education:** Ensuring patients understand their condition, how to use inhalers correctly, and the importance of adherence to treatment.
- **Asthma action plan:** A written plan developed with the healthcare provider detailing daily management and how to handle worsening symptoms.
- **Environmental control:** Minimizing exposure to identified allergens and irritants.
- **Regular monitoring:** Routine follow-up visits to assess asthma control and adjust treatment as needed.
- **Vaccination:** Annual influenza vaccination and pneumococcal vaccination to prevent respiratory infections.

DISCUSSION QUESTIONS

- How do environmental factors contribute to the development and exacerbation of asthma in different populations?
- Discuss the impact of personalized asthma management plans on patient outcomes and quality of life.

MODULE TWO

LESSON ONE: CHRONIC OBSTRUCTIVE PULMONARY DISEASE (COPD): CAUSES, SYMPTOMS, AND MANAGEMENT

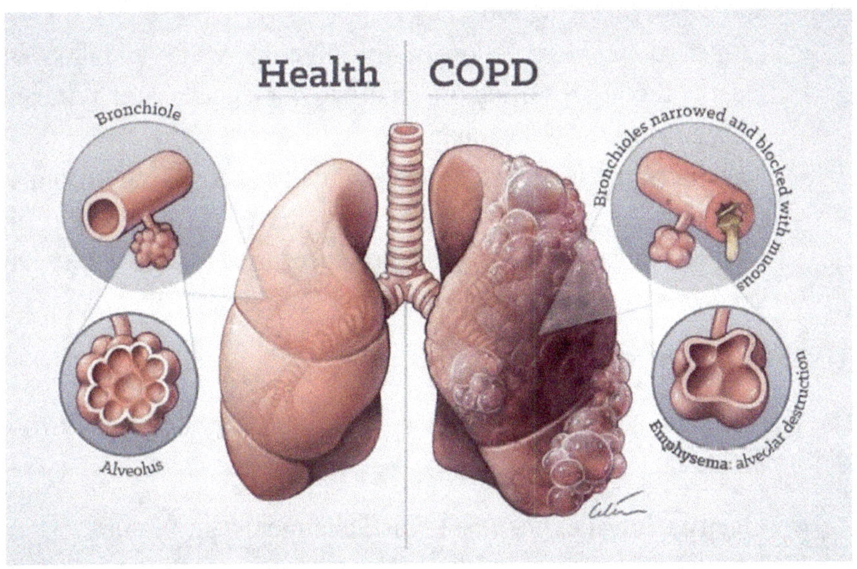

Chronic obstructive pulmonary disease (COPD) is a progressive and debilitating condition characterized by persistent airflow limitation. It encompasses two main components: chronic bronchitis and emphysema. COPD is primarily caused by long-term exposure to harmful particles or gases, with smoking being the most significant risk factor.

EPIDEMIOLOGY

COPD is a major cause of morbidity and mortality worldwide. According to the Global Initiative for Chronic Obstructive Lung Disease (GOLD), COPD affects approximately 384 million people globally and is the third leading cause of death. The prevalence and burden of COPD are expected to increase due to continued exposure to risk factors and an aging population.

PATHOPHYSIOLOGY

The pathophysiology of COPD involves chronic inflammation and structural changes in the airways and lung parenchyma. Key features include:

- Chronic bronchitis: Characterized by chronic inflammation of the bronchi, leading to increased mucus production, cough, and airway obstruction.
- Emphysema: Destruction of the alveolar walls and loss of elastic recoil, resulting in enlarged air spaces and reduced surface area for gas exchange.
- The recruitment of inflammatory cells such as neutrophils, macrophages, and T-lymphocytes drives inflammation in COPD. These cells release proteases and reactive oxygen species, causing tissue damage and remodeling.

RISK FACTORS

The primary risk factor for COPD is smoking. Other significant risk factors include:

- **Occupational exposures:** Dust, chemicals, and fumes.
- **Air pollution:** Both outdoor and indoor air pollution, such as biomass fuel exposure.
- **Genetic factors:** Alpha-1 antitrypsin deficiency is a known genetic risk factor.
- **Age:** The risk of COPD increases with age.
- **Respiratory infections:** Frequent lower respiratory infections during childhood.

CLINICAL MANIFESTATIONS

COPD symptoms typically develop slowly and worsen over time. Common symptoms include:

- **Chronic cough**: Often the first symptom, usually worse in the morning.

- **Sputum production**: Increased mucus production, which may be purulent during exacerbations.
- **Dyspnea:** Progressive shortness of breath, initially with exertion and eventually at rest.
- **Wheezing and chest tightness** May be present but are less prominent than in asthma.
- **Fatigue and weight loss:** Common in advanced stages of the disease.

DIAGNOSIS

Diagnosis of COPD involves a combination of clinical evaluation, lung function testing, and imaging studies. Key diagnostic tools include:

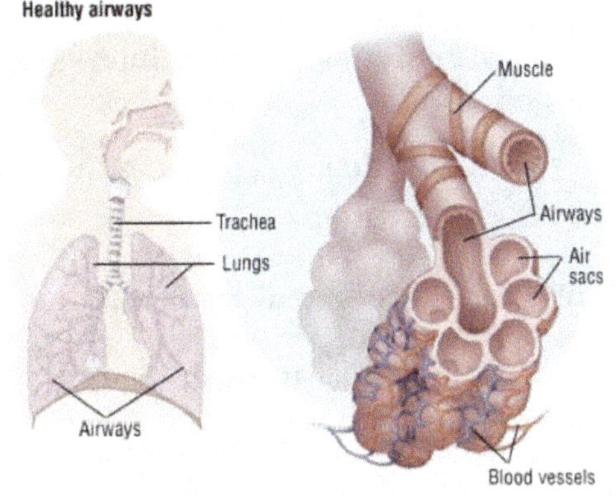

- **Spirometry:** The gold standard for diagnosing COPD, showing a reduced FEV1/FVC ratio (less than 70% post-bronchodilator).
- **Chest X-ray:** Can reveal hyperinflation and other characteristic changes.
- **CT scan:** This procedure provides detailed images of the lung parenchyma and airways, useful for assessing the extent of emphysema.
- **Arterial blood gases:** To assess oxygenation and acid-base status in advanced disease.

MANAGEMENT

The management of COPD is aimed at relieving symptoms, improving quality of life, preventing disease progression, and reducing exacerbations.

Pharmacological Treatment

- **Bronchodilators:** The mainstay of COPD treatment, including short-acting (SABAs and SAMAs) and long-acting bronchodilators (LABAs and LAMAs).
- **Inhaled corticosteroids (ICS):** Used in combination with long-acting bronchodilators in patients with frequent exacerbations.
- **Phosphodiesterase-4 inhibitors**, Such as roflumilast, are used to reduce exacerbations in severe COPD with chronic bronchitis.
- **Mucolytics:** To reduce sputum viscosity and improve clearance.
- **Antibiotics:** For treating bacterial infections during exacerbations.

Non-Pharmacological Strategies

- **Smoking cessation:** The most effective intervention to slow disease progression.
- **Pulmonary rehabilitation:** A comprehensive program including exercise training, education, and nutritional support.
- **Oxygen therapy:** For patients with severe resting hypoxemia.
- **Vaccination:** Annual influenza and pneumococcal vaccines to prevent respiratory infections.
- **Surgical interventions:** Lung volume reduction surgery and lung transplantation in select patients with advanced COPD.

EXACERBATIONS

COPD exacerbations are acute worsening of symptoms that require additional treatment. Respiratory infections often trigger them but can also be caused by environmental pollutants and other factors. Management includes:

- **Short-acting bronchodilators**: Increased use of SABAs and SAMAs.
- **Systemic corticosteroids:** To reduce inflammation.

- **Antibiotics:** For bacterial infections.
- **Hospitalization:** For severe exacerbations requiring intensive treatment and monitoring.

PROGNOSIS

The prognosis of COPD varies depending on the severity of the disease, the presence of comorbidities, and the effectiveness of management strategies. Early diagnosis and intervention, particularly smoking cessation, can significantly improve outcomes. However, COPD remains a progressive and incurable disease, leading to significant morbidity and mortality.

FUTURE DIRECTIONS

Research in COPD is focused on understanding the underlying mechanisms of the disease, developing new treatments, and improving diagnostic tools. Advances in personalized medicine, including the use of biomarkers and genetic profiling, hold promise for more tailored and effective therapies.

DISCUSSION QUESTIONS

- What are the main differences between emphysema and chronic bronchitis in the context of COPD?
- How can healthcare providers effectively promote smoking cessation among patients with COPD?

LESSON TWO: PNEUMONIA: DIAGNOSIS, TREATMENT, AND PREVENTION

Pneumonia is an acute infection of the lung parenchyma that results in inflammation and consolidation of lung tissue. It can be caused by a variety of pathogens, including bacteria, viruses, fungi, and parasites. Pneumonia is a leading cause of morbidity and mortality worldwide, particularly among young children, the elderly, and individuals with compromised immune systems.

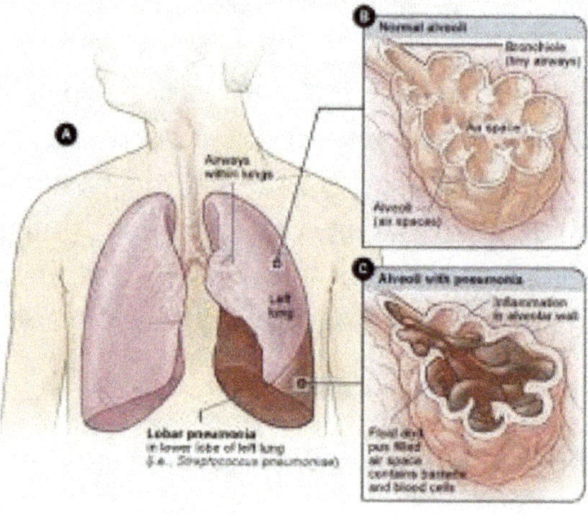

EPIDEMIOLOGY

Pneumonia affects millions of people globally each year, with a significant burden on healthcare systems. According to the World Health Organization (WHO), pneumonia is the leading cause of death in children under five years old. It also poses a considerable risk to older adults and individuals with chronic health conditions. The incidence of pneumonia varies by region, with higher rates in developing countries due to factors such as malnutrition, lack of access to healthcare, and higher prevalence of risk factors like HIV/AIDS.

PATHOPHYSIOLOGY

The pathophysiology of pneumonia involves pathogens invading the lung parenchyma and leading to an inflammatory response. The alveoli fill with fluid and pus, resulting in impaired gas exchange and the clinical manifestations of pneumonia. The type of pathogen and the host's immune response determine the severity and progression of the disease.

Common Pathogens

- **Bacterial:** Streptococcus pneumoniae, Haemophilus influenzae, Mycoplasma pneumoniae, Legionella pneumophila, and Staphylococcus aureus.
- **Viral:** Influenza virus, respiratory syncytial virus (RSV), coronaviruses, adenoviruses.
- **Fungal:** Histoplasma capsulatum, Coccidioides species, and Pneumocystis jirovecii (especially in immunocompromised patients).

CLINICAL MANIFESTATIONS

Pneumonia can present with a variety of symptoms, ranging from mild to severe. Common symptoms include:

- **Fever:** Often high and accompanied by chills.
- **Cough:** Can be productive with purulent or blood-tinged sputum.
- **Dyspnea:** Shortness of breath, which can be severe in extensive pneumonia.
- **Chest pain:** Pleuritic chest pain, worsening with deep breaths or coughing.
- **Fatigue and malaise:** General feeling of unwellness and low energy.
- **Tachypnea and tachycardia:** Rapid breathing and heart rate as the body attempts to maintain oxygenation.

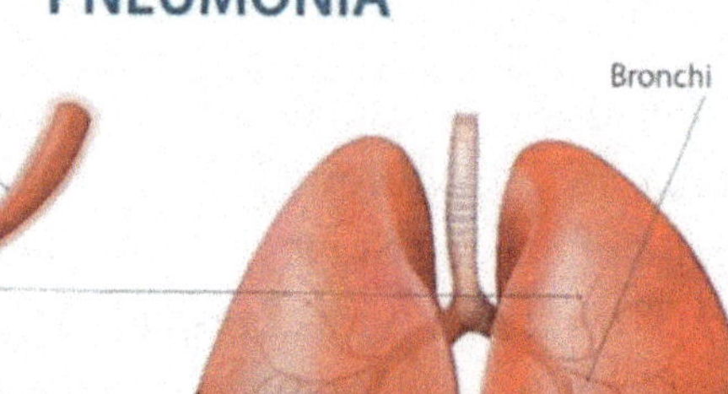

Diagnosing pneumonia involves a combination of clinical assessment, imaging studies, and laboratory tests. Key diagnostic steps include:

- **Clinical evaluation:** History taking and physical examination, looking for signs such as fever, tachypnea, crackles, and decreased breath sounds.
- **Chest X-ray:** This is essential for confirming the diagnosis and assessing the extent of lung involvement. It can show lobar consolidation, interstitial infiltrates, or pleural effusions.
- **Sputum culture:** To identify the causative pathogen and guide antibiotic therapy.
- **Blood tests:** Complete blood count (CBC), blood cultures, and inflammatory markers like C-reactive protein (CRP) and procalcitonin.
- **Pulse oximetry and arterial blood gases:** To assess oxygenation and respiratory function.

MANAGEMENT

The management of pneumonia involves both supportive care and targeted antimicrobial therapy tailored to the likely pathogen and patient-specific factors.

Antimicrobial Therapy

- **Empirical antibiotics:** Initially based on the most likely pathogens and local antibiotic resistance patterns. Common choices include macrolides, fluoroquinolones, or beta-lactam antibiotics.
- **Pathogen-specific therapy:** Adjusted based on culture results and sensitivities.
- **Antiviral therapy:** For viral pneumonia, such as oseltamivir for influenza.

SUPPORTIVE CARE

- **Oxygen therapy:** To maintain adequate oxygenation in hypoxemic patients.
- **Fluids and electrolytes**: Ensuring proper hydration and electrolyte balance.
- **Antipyretics:** For fever and discomfort.
- **Mechanical ventilation:** In severe cases with respiratory failure.

PREVENTION

Preventing pneumonia involves vaccination, hygiene measures, and addressing risk factors.

- **Vaccination:** Pneumococcal vaccines (PCV13 and PPSV23) and annual influenza vaccination are crucial in preventing bacterial and viral pneumonia.
- **Hand hygiene:** Regular hand washing to reduce the spread of pathogens.
- **Smoking cessation:** Reducing the risk of respiratory infections.

- **Healthy lifestyle:** Good nutrition, regular exercise, and managing chronic conditions to enhance overall immune function.

COMPLICATIONS

Pneumonia can lead to various complications, especially in high-risk individuals. These include:

- **Pleural effusion:** Accumulation of fluid in the pleural space.
- **Empyema:** Collection of pus in the pleural cavity.
- **Lung abscess:** Formation of a cavity filled with pus in the lung.
- **Sepsis:** A severe systemic response to infection that can lead to organ failure.
- **Acute respiratory distress syndrome (ARDS):** Severe inflammation and fluid buildup in the alveoli, leading to critical hypoxemia.

PROGNOSIS

The prognosis of pneumonia depends on several factors, including the patient's age, underlying health conditions, the causative pathogen, and the timeliness and appropriateness of treatment. While many individuals recover fully with appropriate treatment, severe cases can lead to prolonged illness, complications, or death, particularly in vulnerable populations.

DISCUSSION QUESTIONS

- Compare and contrast the treatment protocols for community-acquired pneumonia (CAP) and hospital-acquired pneumonia (HAP).
- Discuss the role of vaccination in preventing pneumonia in at-risk populations.

LESSON ONE: LUNG CANCER: AN IN-DEPTH ANALYSIS

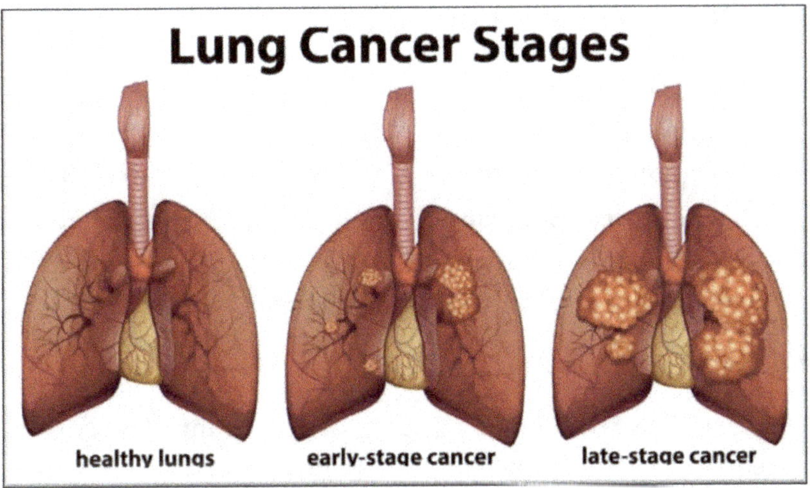

Lung cancer is one of the most common and deadliest forms of cancer worldwide. It arises from the epithelial cells of the respiratory tract and is broadly classified into non-small cell lung cancer (NSCLC) and small cell lung cancer (SCLC). Early detection and advances in treatment have improved outcomes, but the overall prognosis remains poor due to the aggressive nature of the disease and late-stage diagnosis in many cases.

EPIDEMIOLOGY

Lung cancer is the leading cause of cancer-related deaths globally. According to the World Health Organization (WHO), it accounts for approximately 1.8 million deaths annually. The incidence and mortality rates vary widely by region, reflecting differences in smoking prevalence, air pollution, and access to healthcare.

RISK FACTORS

The primary risk factor for lung cancer is tobacco smoking, which is responsible for about 85% of cases. Other significant risk factors include:

- **Secondhand smoke:** Exposure to tobacco smoke from others.
- **Radon gas:** A naturally occurring radioactive gas found in homes and buildings.
- **Occupational exposures:** Asbestos, silica, and other carcinogens.
- **Air pollution:** Particularly fine particulate matter (PM2.5).
- **Genetic predisposition:** Family history of lung cancer.
- **Previous lung diseases**, Such as chronic obstructive pulmonary disease (COPD) and pulmonary fibrosis.

PATHOPHYSIOLOGY

Lung cancer develops through a series of genetic mutations that lead to uncontrolled cell growth. The two main types of lung cancer, NSCLC and SCLC, have distinct biological behaviors and responses to treatment:

- **Non-Small Cell Lung Cancer (NSCLC):** Comprises about 85% of lung cancer cases and includes adenocarcinoma, squamous cell carcinoma, and large cell carcinoma.
- **Small Cell Lung Cancer (SCLC)** accounts for about 15% of cases and is characterized by rapid growth and early metastasis.

CLINICAL MANIFESTATIONS

Lung cancer symptoms often appear late in the disease course and can include:

- **Persistent cough:** Often worsening over time.
- **Hemoptysis:** Coughing up blood.
- **Chest pain:** Pain that may be dull, aching, or sharp.
- **Shortness of breath:** Due to obstruction or pleural effusion.

- **Unexplained weight loss**: Common in advanced cancer.
- **Fatigue and weakness:** General feeling of being unwell.

DIAGNOSIS

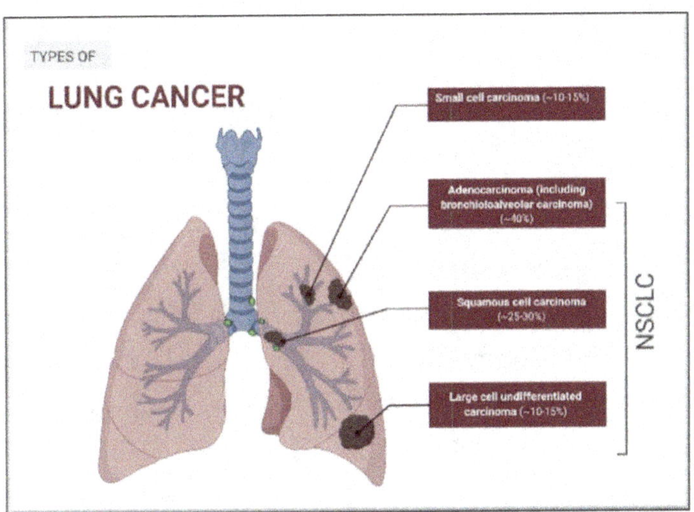

Diagnosing lung cancer involves imaging studies, tissue biopsy, and molecular testing. Key diagnostic steps include:

- **Chest X-ray and CT scan:** Initial imaging to detect lung masses and assess the extent of disease.
- **Bronchoscopy:** Visualization and biopsy of the airways.
- **Needle biopsy:** Obtaining tissue samples from lung masses.
- **PET scan:** To evaluate for metastasis.
- **Molecular testing:** Identifying specific genetic mutations and markers that guide targeted therapy (e.g., EGFR, ALK, PD-L1).

STAGING

Lung cancer staging, based on the TNM system (Tumor, Node, Metastasis), is crucial for determining prognosis and guiding treatment:

- **Stage I:** Localized disease.
- **Stage II:** Involvement of nearby lymph nodes.
- **Stage III**: Spread to regional lymph nodes and structures.
- **Stage IV:** Distant metastasis.

MANAGEMENT

The treatment of lung cancer depends on the type, stage, and molecular characteristics of the tumor, as well as the patient's overall health.

Surgery

- **Lobectomy:** Removal of a lobe of the lung.
- **Pneumonectomy:** Removal of an entire lung.
- **Segmentectomy or wedge resection:** Removal of a smaller portion of the lung.

Radiation Therapy

- **External beam radiation:** Targeting the tumor with high-energy beams.
- **Stereotactic body radiotherapy (SBRT):** Precise radiation delivery for small tumors.

Chemotherapy

- **Platinum-based regimens:** Commonly used for both NSCLC and SCLC.
- **Adjuvant and neoadjuvant chemotherapy:** Used before or after surgery to reduce recurrence.

PREVENTION

Preventing lung cancer involves reducing exposure to known risk factors and implementing early detection strategies.

Smoking Cessation

- **Public health campaigns:** Educating the public about the risks of smoking and secondhand smoke.

- **Support programs:** Providing resources and support for individuals trying to quit smoking.
- **Regulations:** Implementing policies to reduce tobacco use, such as increased taxes and smoking bans in public places.

Environmental and Occupational Safety

- **Radon testing:** Identifying and mitigating radon exposure in homes and buildings.
- **Workplace safety:** Reducing exposure to carcinogens through regulations and protective measures.

DISCUSSION QUESTIONS

- What are the benefits and limitations of low-dose CT screening for lung cancer?
- How do different genetic mutations influence the treatment options for non-small cell lung cancer (NSCLC)?

LESSON TWO: TUBERCULOSIS (TB): DIAGNOSIS, TREATMENT, AND CONTROL

Tuberculosis (TB) is a contagious bacterial infection caused by Mycobacterium tuberculosis. Despite being a curable and preventable disease, TB remains a significant global health challenge, particularly in low- and middle-income countries.

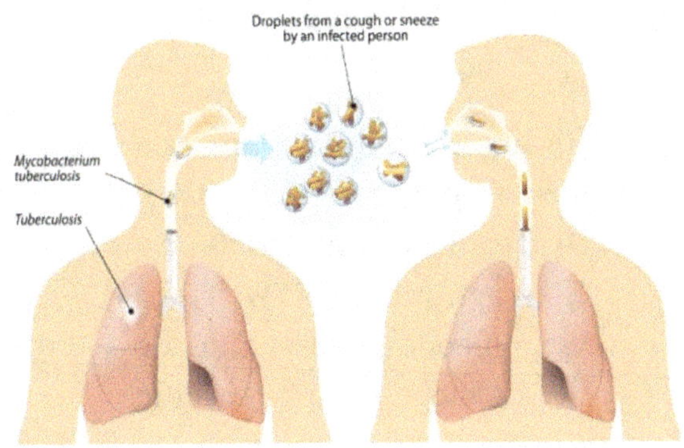

EPIDEMIOLOGY

TB affects millions of people worldwide each year. According to the World Health Organization (WHO), there were approximately 10 million new TB cases and 1.4 million TB-related deaths in 2019. TB incidence is highest in regions with high HIV prevalence, poor healthcare infrastructure, and socioeconomic challenges.

PATHOPHYSIOLOGY

TB is primarily transmitted through the inhalation of airborne droplets from an infected person. Once inhaled, M. tuberculosis can reach the alveoli, where macrophages ingest it. The bacteria can evade the immune response and remain dormant or multiply and cause active disease. The progression of TB involves:

- **Latent TB infection (LTBI):** The bacteria are present in the body but are inactive and do not cause symptoms. LTBI can reactivate, particularly in individuals with weakened immune systems.
- **Active TB disease:** The bacteria multiply, causing symptoms and the potential to spread to others.

CLINICAL MANIFESTATIONS

The symptoms of TB can vary depending on the site of infection but typically include:

- **Pulmonary TB:** Cough lasting more than three weeks, hemoptysis (coughing up blood), chest pain, weight loss, night sweats, fever, and fatigue.
- **Extrapulmonary TB:** TB can affect other organs, such as the lymph nodes, bones, kidneys, and the central nervous system, leading to symptoms specific to the affected site.

DIAGNOSIS

Diagnosing TB involves a combination of clinical evaluation, microbiological tests, and imaging studies.

Microbiological Tests

- Sputum smear microscopy: Detecting acid-fast bacilli (AFB) in sputum samples.
- Culture: Growing M. tuberculosis from clinical samples is considered the gold standard.
- Molecular tests: Rapid tests such as Xpert MTB/RIF detect TB DNA and resistance to rifampicin.

IMAGING

- Chest X-ray: Helps identify characteristic patterns of pulmonary TB, such as cavities and infiltrates.

TUBERCULIN SKIN TEST (TST) AND INTERFERON-GAMMA RELEASE ASSAYS (IGRAS)

- TST: Involves injecting purified protein derivative (PPD) and measuring the skin reaction.
- IGRAs: Blood tests that measure the immune response to TB antigens, used primarily for diagnosing LTBI.

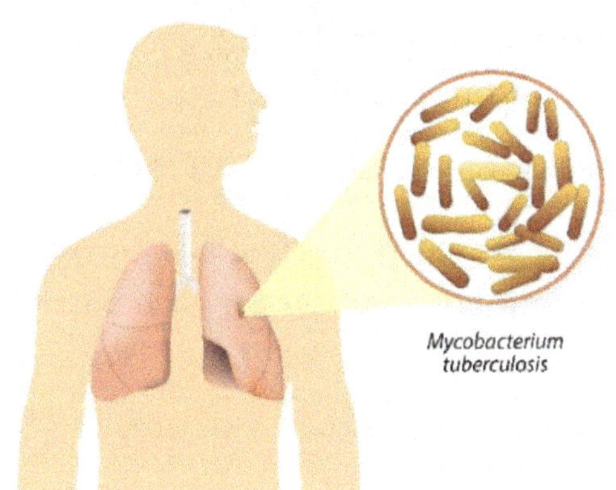

TREATMENT

The treatment of TB involves prolonged antibiotic therapy, typically lasting six months or longer, to ensure complete eradication of the bacteria and prevent resistance.

- First-Line Anti-TB Drugs
- Isoniazid (INH)
- Rifampicin (RIF)
- Pyrazinamide (PZA)
- Ethambutol (EMB)

TREATMENT REGIMENS

- Initial phase: Intensive treatment with four drugs (INH, RIF, PZA, EMB) for two months.
- Continuation phase: Treatment with INH and RIF for an additional four months.

DRUG-RESISTANT TB

- Multidrug-resistant TB (MDR-TB): Resistant to at least INH and RIF, requiring second-line drugs and a longer treatment duration.
- Extensively drug-resistant TB (XDR-TB): Resistant to first-line drugs and some second-line drugs, posing significant treatment challenges.

CONTROL AND PREVENTION

Controlling and preventing TB involves a combination of public health measures, vaccination, and addressing social determinants of health.

PUBLIC HEALTH MEASURES

- Active case finding: Screening high-risk populations and contacts of TB patients.
- Directly observed treatment (DOT): Ensuring patients adhere to their treatment regimen through supervised administration of medications.

VACCINATION

- BCG vaccine: This vaccine protects against severe forms of TB in children, but its efficacy in preventing pulmonary TB in adults is limited.

ADDRESSING SOCIAL DETERMINANTS

- Improving living conditions: Reducing overcrowding and improving ventilation.
- Addressing malnutrition: Ensuring adequate nutrition to strengthen the immune system.
- Reducing stigma: Encouraging individuals to seek treatment without fear of discrimination.

FUTURE DIRECTIONS

Research in TB is focused on developing new diagnostics, vaccines, and treatments. Areas of active investigation include:

- Shorter treatment regimens: Reducing the duration of TB treatment to improve adherence and outcomes.
- New vaccines: Developing more effective vaccines for both prevention and therapeutic purposes.
- Host-directed therapies: Targeting the host's immune response to enhance the effectiveness of TB treatment.

DISCUSSION QUESTIONS

- What measures can be taken to reduce the incidence of occupational asthma in high-risk industries?
- Discuss the long-term health effects of exposure to indoor air pollutants in urban environments.

LESSON ONE: INTERSTITIAL LUNG DISEASE (ILD): A COMPREHENSIVE OVERVIEW

Interstitial lung diseases (ILD) are a group of disorders characterized by inflammation and fibrosis of the lung interstitium, leading to impaired gas exchange and progressive lung dysfunction. ILDs include a variety of conditions, such as idiopathic pulmonary fibrosis (IPF), sarcoidosis, and connective tissue disease-associated ILD.

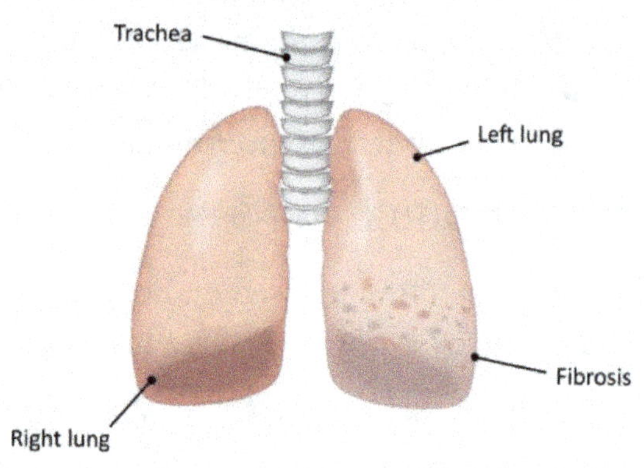

EPIDEMIOLOGY

The prevalence of ILD varies depending on the specific disease. Idiopathic pulmonary fibrosis (IPF) is one of the most common and severe forms, with an estimated prevalence of 14-43 cases per 100,000 people in the United States and Europe. The incidence and prevalence of other ILDs are less well-defined but are significant contributors to chronic respiratory disease.

PATHOPHYSIOLOGY

The pathophysiology of ILD involves a complex interplay of genetic, environmental, and immune factors that lead to lung inflammation and fibrosis. Key mechanisms include:

- Inflammation: Initial injury to the alveoli triggers an inflammatory response involving immune cells such as macrophages and lymphocytes.
- Fibrosis: Chronic inflammation activates fibroblasts and excessively deposits extracellular matrix proteins, resulting in scarring and thickening of the lung interstitium.
- Impaired gas exchange: Fibrosis disrupts the architecture of the alveoli, impairing oxygen transfer and leading to progressive respiratory insufficiency.

RISK FACTORS

The risk factors for ILD vary depending on the specific disease but can include:

- Environmental exposures: Occupational exposures to dust, chemicals, and organic materials (e.g., asbestos, silica, bird droppings).
- Smoking: Increases the risk of several forms of ILD, including IPF.
- Autoimmune diseases: Conditions such as rheumatoid arthritis, scleroderma, and lupus can be associated with ILD.
- Genetic predisposition: Family history of ILD and specific genetic mutations.

CLINICAL MANIFESTATIONS

The symptoms of ILD are often non-specific and can include:

- Dyspnea: Progressive shortness of breath, initially with exertion and eventually at rest.
- Chronic cough: Typically dry and persistent.
- Fatigue: Generalized tiredness and lack of energy.
- Weight loss: Unintentional loss of weight.
- Clubbing: Enlargement of the fingertips, seen in some cases of advanced disease.

DIAGNOSIS

Diagnosing ILD involves a combination of clinical evaluation, imaging studies, pulmonary function tests, and sometimes lung biopsy.

IMAGING

- High-resolution CT (HRCT) scan: This is the gold standard for imaging ILD. It provides detailed images of the lung parenchyma and identifies patterns of fibrosis.

PULMONARY FUNCTION TESTS (PFTS)

- Spirometry: Measures lung volumes and airflow, often showing a restrictive pattern (reduced total lung capacity).
- Diffusing capacity for carbon monoxide (DLCO): This assesses the lungs' ability to transfer gas, which is typically reduced in ILD.

LUNG BIOPSY

- Surgical biopsy: Sometimes necessary to obtain a definitive diagnosis, especially in cases where the HRCT pattern is not typical.

MANAGEMENT

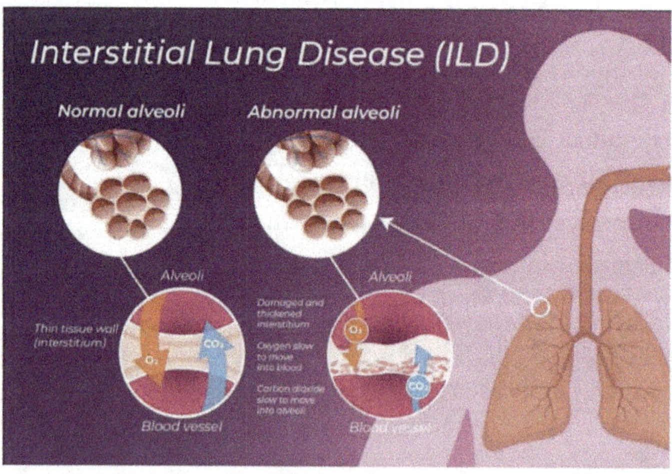

The management of ILD focuses on relieving symptoms, slowing disease progression, and managing complications. The approach varies depending on the specific type of ILD and its severity.

Pharmacological Treatments

- Anti-fibrotic agents: Medications such as pirfenidone and nintedanib are specifically approved for idiopathic pulmonary fibrosis (IPF) and work by slowing the progression of fibrosis.
- Immunosuppressive therapy: Drugs like corticosteroids, azathioprine, and mycophenolate mofetil are used in ILDs associated with autoimmune diseases or significant inflammation.
- Proton pump inhibitors (PPIs): Used to treat gastroesophageal reflux disease (GERD), which is commonly associated with ILD and may exacerbate lung disease.

Non-Pharmacological Treatments

- Oxygen therapy: Supplemental oxygen to maintain adequate oxygen levels and relieve dyspnea.
- Pulmonary rehabilitation: A comprehensive program that includes exercise training, education, and support to improve the physical and emotional well-being of patients.
- Lung transplantation: Considered for patients with advanced ILD who are refractory to medical therapy.

PROGNOSIS

The prognosis of ILD varies widely depending on the specific disease and its progression. For example, IPF has a median survival of 3-5 years from diagnosis, while other forms of ILD associated with autoimmune diseases may have a more variable course. Early diagnosis and appropriate management are crucial for improving outcomes.

PREVENTION AND MONITORING

- Avoidance of environmental exposures: Reducing contact with known occupational and environmental triggers.
- Regular monitoring: Routine follow-up with pulmonary function tests, imaging, and clinical assessments to track disease progression and adjust treatment as needed.

DISCUSSION QUESTIONS

- Discuss the role of high-resolution CT in the diagnosis of various interstitial lung diseases.
- How can anti-fibrotic therapies alter the prognosis for patients with idiopathic pulmonary fibrosis (IPF)?

LESSON TWO: PEDIATRIC RESPIRATORY DISEASES: A COMPREHENSIVE GUIDE

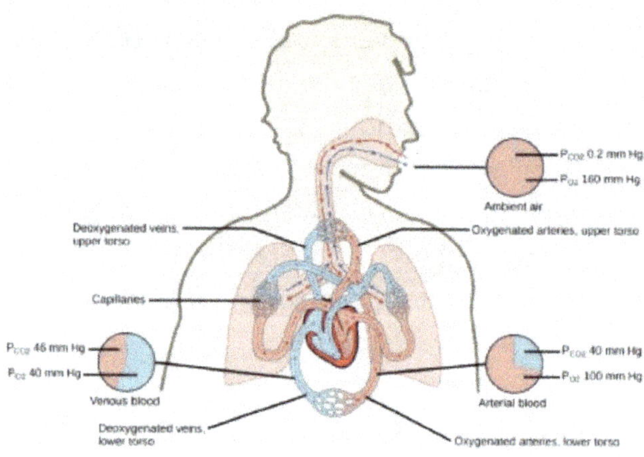

Pediatric respiratory diseases encompass a wide range of conditions affecting the respiratory system in infants, children, and adolescents. These diseases can significantly impact growth, development, and quality of life. This lesson will cover common pediatric respiratory conditions, their causes, symptoms, and management strategies.

EPIDEMIOLOGY

Respiratory diseases are among the most common reasons for pediatric medical visits and hospitalizations. Conditions such as asthma, bronchiolitis, and pneumonia are particularly prevalent. The incidence and prevalence of these diseases vary by age, geographic region, and socioeconomic status.

COMMON PEDIATRIC RESPIRATORY DISEASES

Asthma

Asthma is a chronic inflammatory disease of the airways characterized by recurrent episodes of wheezing, breathlessness, chest tightness, and coughing. It is one of the most common chronic diseases in children.

- Causes: Genetic predisposition, environmental triggers (allergens, pollution), respiratory infections, and lifestyle factors.
- Symptoms: Wheezing, shortness of breath, chest tightness, and coughing, especially at night or early morning.
- Management: Inhaled corticosteroids, bronchodilators, allergen avoidance, and asthma action plans.

Bronchiolitis

Bronchiolitis is a viral infection of the small airways (bronchioles) primarily affecting infants and young children. It is most commonly caused by the respiratory syncytial virus (RSV).

- Causes: RSV and other viruses such as rhinovirus, influenza, and parainfluenza.
- Symptoms: Cough, wheezing, rapid breathing, and difficulty feeding.
- Management: Supportive care, including hydration, oxygen therapy, and, in severe cases, mechanical ventilation.

Pneumonia

Pneumonia is an infection of the lung parenchyma and can be caused by bacteria, viruses, or fungi.

- Causes: Streptococcus pneumoniae, Haemophilus influenzae, respiratory viruses.
- Symptoms: Fever, cough, rapid breathing, chest pain, and fatigue.
- Management: Antibiotics for bacterial pneumonia, antiviral medications for viral pneumonia, supportive care.

Cystic Fibrosis

Cystic fibrosis (CF) is a genetic disorder that affects the respiratory and digestive systems. It is characterized by the production of thick, sticky mucus that can clog the airways and lead to recurrent lung infections.

- Causes: Mutations in the CFTR gene.
- Symptoms: Chronic cough, frequent lung infections, wheezing, and digestive issues.
- Management: Airway clearance techniques, inhaled medications, antibiotics, and pancreatic enzyme replacement.

DIAGNOSTIC APPROACHES

Diagnosing pediatric respiratory diseases involves a thorough clinical evaluation, including history taking, physical examination, and various diagnostic tests.

- History and Physical Examination: Assessing symptoms, family history, environmental exposures, and physical signs such as wheezing or crackles.
- Imaging: Chest X-rays and CT scans to visualize lung structures and detect abnormalities.
- Pulmonary Function Tests: Spirometry to measure lung function, particularly in older children who can perform the tests reliably.

- Laboratory Tests: Blood tests, sputum cultures, and genetic testing for conditions like cystic fibrosis.

MANAGEMENT STRATEGIES

The management of pediatric respiratory diseases involves a combination of pharmacological treatments, supportive care, and preventive measures.

Pharmacological Treatments

- Asthma: Inhaled corticosteroids, bronchodilators, leukotriene modifiers.
- Infections: Antibiotics for bacterial infections, antiviral drugs for viral infections.
- Cystic Fibrosis: Mucolytics, inhaled antibiotics, CFTR modulators.

Supportive Care

- Oxygen Therapy: To maintain adequate oxygenation in hypoxemic patients.
- Hydration and Nutrition: Ensuring proper fluid and nutritional intake is especially important in conditions like cystic fibrosis.
- Respiratory Support: Non-invasive ventilation or mechanical ventilation in severe cases.

Preventive Measures

- Vaccinations: Immunizations against common respiratory pathogens such as influenza, pneumococcus, and pertussis.
- Avoidance of Triggers: Reducing exposure to allergens, tobacco smoke, and pollutants.
- Education and Self-Management: Teaching patients and families about disease management, recognizing symptoms, and implementing action plans.

PROGNOSIS

The prognosis of pediatric respiratory diseases varies widely. While many conditions, such as mild asthma or viral bronchiolitis, have good outcomes with appropriate management, others, like cystic fibrosis, require lifelong care and can significantly impact the quality of life and life expectancy.

FUTURE DIRECTIONS

Research in pediatric respiratory diseases aims to improve diagnostic techniques, develop new treatments, and enhance preventive strategies. Key areas of focus include:

- Genetic and Molecular Research: Understanding the genetic basis of diseases like cystic fibrosis and asthma to develop targeted therapies.
- Innovative Therapies: Exploring new medications, gene therapy, and novel delivery systems for respiratory drugs.
- Preventive Strategies: Developing vaccines and public health initiatives to reduce the incidence of respiratory infections.

DISCUSSION QUESTIONS

- What are the primary differences in the presentation of respiratory infections between children and adults?
- How can pediatric asthma management be tailored to ensure adherence and effective control in young patients?

MODULE FIVE

LESSON ONE: ALLERGIC RESPIRATORY DISEASES: UNDERSTANDING AND MANAGEMENT

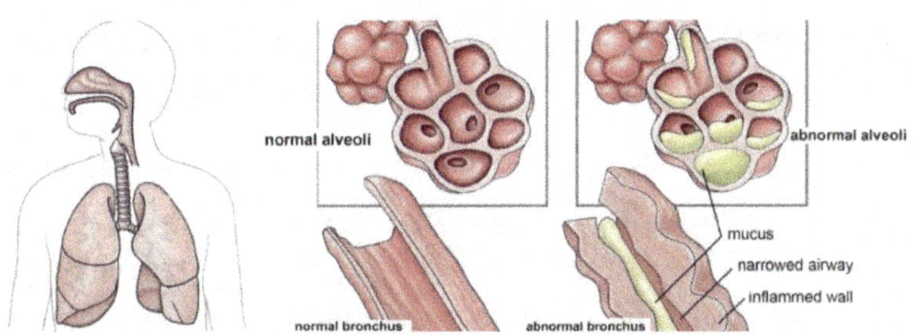

Allergic respiratory diseases result from the immune system's response to allergens, leading to conditions like allergic rhinitis and allergic asthma. This chapter will cover the causes, symptoms, and management of these conditions.

ALLERGIC RIIINITIS

Allergic rhinitis, also known as hay fever, is an allergic reaction that causes sneezing, congestion, and a runny nose.

- Causes: Pollen, dust mites, pet dander, mold, and other allergens.
- Symptoms: Sneezing, runny or stuffy nose, itchy eyes, nose, and throat.
- Management: Avoiding allergens, using antihistamines, nasal corticosteroids, and decongestants.

ALLERGIC ASTHMA

Allergic asthma is triggered by exposure to allergens, leading to asthma symptoms.

- Causes: Pollen, dust mites, mold, pet dander, and other allergens.

- Symptoms: Wheezing, coughing, chest tightness, and shortness of breath.
- Management: Avoiding allergens, using inhaled corticosteroids, bronchodilators, and leukotriene modifiers.

DIAGNOSIS

Diagnosing allergic respiratory diseases involves a combination of medical history, physical examination, and allergy testing.

- Medical History: Identifying potential allergens and correlating them with symptoms.
- Physical Examination: Checking for signs of allergic reactions, such as nasal inflammation and wheezing.
- Allergy Testing: Skin prick tests and blood tests to identify specific allergens.

PREVENTION AND MANAGEMENT

Preventing and managing allergic respiratory diseases involves reducing exposure to allergens and using medications to control symptoms.

- Avoidance: Keeping windows closed during high pollen seasons, using air purifiers, and regularly cleaning to reduce dust and pet dander.
- Medications: Antihistamines, nasal corticosteroids, decongestants, and asthma medications.
- Immunotherapy: Allergy shots or sublingual tablets to gradually desensitize the immune system to specific allergens.

FUTURE DIRECTIONS

Research in allergic respiratory diseases focuses on understanding the immune response to allergens, developing new treatments, and improving prevention strategies.

- Biologics: Developing targeted therapies to block specific immune pathways involved in allergic reactions.

- Genetic Research: Understanding genetic predispositions to allergies and asthma to develop personalized treatments.
- Environmental Interventions: Creating more effective ways to reduce environmental allergens.

DISCUSSION QUESTIONS

- How do allergen immunotherapy and pharmacotherapy differ in managing allergic rhinitis and asthma?
- What are the challenges in diagnosing and managing food-induced respiratory allergic reactions?

LESSON TWO: RESPIRATORY INFECTIONS: DIAGNOSIS AND TREATMENT

Respiratory infections are a leading cause of morbidity and mortality worldwide. This lesson will cover common respiratory infections, their diagnosis, and treatment.

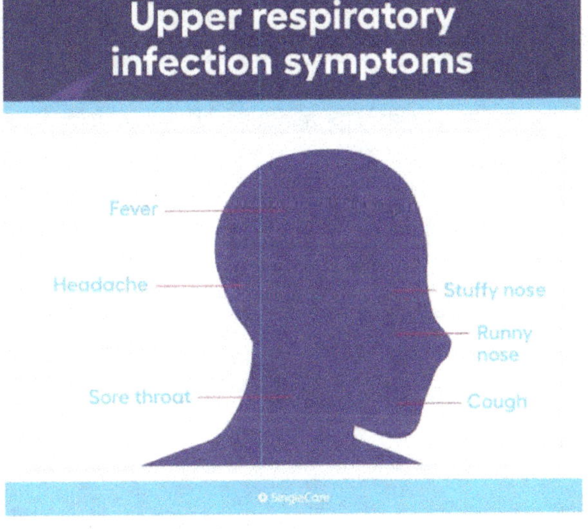

COMMON RESPIRATORY INFECTIONS

Influenza

Influenza, or the flu, is a viral infection that affects the respiratory system.

- Causes: Influenza virus types A, B, and C.
- Symptoms: Fever, chills, cough, sore throat, body aches, fatigue, and headache.

- Management: Antiviral medications (oseltamivir, zanamivir), rest, hydration, and symptomatic treatment.

Pneumonia

Pneumonia is an infection of the lungs that bacteria, viruses, or fungi can cause.

- Causes: Streptococcus pneumoniae, Haemophilus influenzae, respiratory viruses, fungi.
- Symptoms: Fever, cough, shortness of breath, chest pain, fatigue.
- Management: Antibiotics for bacterial pneumonia, antiviral medications for viral pneumonia, antifungal treatments for fungal pneumonia, supportive care.

Tuberculosis

Tuberculosis (TB) is a bacterial infection caused by Mycobacterium tuberculosis.

- Causes: Mycobacterium tuberculosis.
- Symptoms: Persistent cough, hemoptysis, weight loss, night sweats, fever.
- Management: Long-term antibiotic therapy with drugs like isoniazid, rifampin, pyrazinamide, and ethambutol.

DIAGNOSIS

Diagnosing respiratory infections involves clinical evaluation, laboratory tests, and imaging studies.

- Clinical Evaluation: Assessing symptoms and physical signs of infection.
- Laboratory Tests: Blood tests, sputum cultures, rapid antigen tests, polymerase chain reaction (PCR) tests.
- Imaging: Chest X-rays and CT scans to visualize lung involvement.

TREATMENT STRATEGIES

Treatment of respiratory infections depends on the specific pathogen and the severity of the disease.

- Antibiotics: Used for bacterial infections based on culture results and susceptibility testing.
- Antivirals: Used for viral infections, with specific medications targeting different viruses.
- Antifungals: Used for fungal infections, often requiring prolonged treatment.
- Supportive Care: Hydration, rest, oxygen therapy, and mechanical ventilation in severe cases.

PREVENTION

Preventing respiratory infections involves vaccination, good hygiene practices, and public health measures.

- Vaccination: Influenza vaccine, pneumococcal vaccine, tuberculosis vaccine (BCG).
- Hygiene Practices: Handwashing, wearing masks, avoiding close contact with infected individuals.
- Public Health Measures: Quarantine, isolation, and contact tracing during outbreaks.

FUTURE DIRECTIONS

Research in respiratory infections aims to develop new vaccines, improve diagnostic techniques, and discover novel treatments.

- Vaccine Development: Creating more effective and long-lasting vaccines for respiratory pathogens.
- Rapid Diagnostics: Developing faster and more accurate diagnostic tools.
- Antimicrobial Resistance: Addressing the challenge of antibiotic resistance through new drugs and stewardship programs.

- What measures can be taken to reduce the incidence of occupational asthma in high-risk industries?
- Discuss the long-term health effects of exposure to indoor air pollutants in urban environments.

MODULE SIX

LESSON ONE: RESPIRATORY DISORDERS IN THE ELDERLY: CHALLENGES AND MANAGEMENT

Respiratory disorders in the elderly are a significant concern due to age-related changes in the respiratory system and the presence

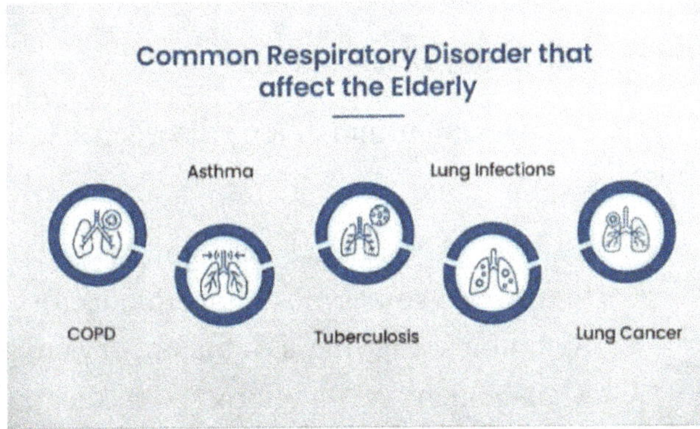

of comorbidities. This chapter will cover common respiratory conditions in the elderly, their management, and challenges.

COMMON RESPIRATORY CONDITIONS IN THE ELDERLY

Chronic Obstructive Pulmonary Disease (COPD)

COPD is a progressive lung disease characterized by airflow obstruction.

- Causes: Smoking, long-term exposure to lung irritants.
- Symptoms: Chronic cough, sputum production, shortness of breath, wheezing.
- Management: Bronchodilators, inhaled corticosteroids, pulmonary rehabilitation, oxygen therapy.

Pneumonia

Pneumonia is a significant cause of morbidity and mortality in the elderly.

- Causes: Bacteria (e.g., Streptococcus pneumoniae), viruses, fungi.
- Symptoms: Fever, cough, shortness of breath, chest pain, confusion.
- Management: Antibiotics, antiviral medications, supportive care, vaccination.

Interstitial Lung Disease (ILD)

ILD encompasses a group of lung disorders causing inflammation and fibrosis.

- Causes: Age-related changes, exposure to environmental toxins, and sometimes idiopathic factors.
- Symptoms: Shortness of breath, dry cough, fatigue.
- Management: Anti-fibrotic medications, corticosteroids, oxygen therapy, pulmonary rehabilitation.

DIAGNOSIS IN THE ELDERLY

Diagnosing respiratory disorders in the elderly can be challenging due to overlapping symptoms with other comorbid conditions and age-related changes in lung function.

- History and Physical Examination: Thorough assessment of symptoms, smoking history, occupational exposures, and physical examination findings.
- Imaging: Chest X-rays and CT scans to detect structural abnormalities and inflammation.
- Pulmonary Function Tests: Spirometry to measure airflow obstruction and lung capacity.
- Laboratory Tests: Blood tests, sputum cultures, and, in some cases, bronchoscopy.

MANAGEMENT STRATEGIES

Managing respiratory disorders in the elderly involves a comprehensive approach that includes pharmacological treatments, lifestyle modifications, and supportive care.

Pharmacological Treatments

Bronchodilators: Used in COPD to relax airway muscles and improve airflow.

- Inhaled Corticosteroids: Reduce inflammation in conditions like asthma and COPD.
- Antibiotics and Antivirals: For bacterial and viral infections, respectively.
- Anti-fibrotic Agents: For interstitial lung diseases to slow disease progression.

Lifestyle Modifications

- Smoking Cessation: Vital for preventing and managing COPD and other respiratory conditions.
- Exercise and Pulmonary Rehabilitation: Enhance physical fitness and respiratory function.
- Nutritional Support: Ensure adequate nutrition to support overall health and immune function.

Supportive Care

- Oxygen Therapy: For patients with chronic hypoxemia to maintain adequate oxygen levels.
- Vaccinations: Annual influenza vaccine and pneumococcal vaccines to prevent respiratory infections.
- Education: Teaching patients and caregivers about disease management, medication adherence, and recognizing symptoms of exacerbations.

CHALLENGES IN MANAGEMENT

Managing respiratory disorders in the elderly comes with unique challenges, including:

- Polypharmacy: The use of multiple medications can lead to drug interactions and adverse effects.

- Comorbidities: Other chronic conditions, such as heart disease, diabetes, and arthritis, can complicate management.
- Cognitive Impairment: Conditions like dementia can affect a patient's ability to adhere to treatment plans and recognize symptoms.
- Frailty: Physical frailty can limit the ability to participate in pulmonary rehabilitation and other physical activities.

FUTURE DIRECTIONS

Research in respiratory disorders in the elderly aims to develop better diagnostic tools, effective treatments, and tailored management strategies.

- Personalized Medicine: Tailoring treatments based on individual genetic profiles and disease characteristics.
- New Therapies: Developing novel medications to address specific pathophysiological processes in elderly patients.
- Technology and Telemedicine: Utilizing telehealth platforms for remote monitoring and management of chronic respiratory conditions.

DISCUSSION QUESTIONS

- How does the aging process affect the presentation and progression of COPD in elderly patients?
- What are the best practices for managing polypharmacy in elderly patients with multiple respiratory disorders?

LESSON TWO: PULMONARY HYPERTENSION: UNDERSTANDING AND MANAGEMENT

Pulmonary hypertension (PH) is a complex condition characterized by elevated blood pressure in the pulmonary

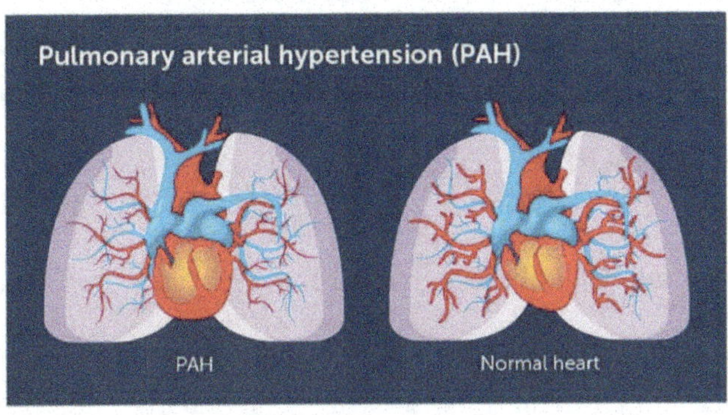

arteries, leading to right heart failure. This chapter will cover the causes, classification, symptoms, diagnosis, and management of pulmonary hypertension.

CAUSES AND CLASSIFICATION

Pulmonary hypertension can be classified into five groups based on underlying causes:

- Group 1: Pulmonary Arterial Hypertension (PAH): Idiopathic, heritable, drug-induced, or associated with conditions like connective tissue diseases and congenital heart diseases.
- Group 2: PH due to Left Heart Disease: Resulting from conditions like left ventricular systolic or diastolic dysfunction and valvular heart disease.
- Group 3: PH due to Lung Diseases and Hypoxia: Associated with COPD, interstitial lung disease, sleep apnea, and chronic exposure to high altitudes.
- Group 4: Chronic Thromboembolic Pulmonary Hypertension (CTEPH): Caused by chronic blood clots in the lungs.
- Group 5: PH with Unclear Multifactorial Mechanisms: Including conditions such as hematologic disorders, systemic disorders, metabolic disorders, and others.

SYMPTOMS

- Early Symptoms: Shortness of breath, fatigue, dizziness, and chest pain, particularly during physical activity.
- Advanced Symptoms include swelling in the ankles, legs, and abdomen, cyanosis, and syncope (fainting).

DIAGNOSIS

Diagnosing pulmonary hypertension involves a comprehensive approach, including clinical evaluation, imaging, and specialized tests.

- Clinical Evaluation: Detailed history and physical examination, focusing on symptoms and risk factors.
- Echocardiography: Initial non-invasive screening to assess right heart function and estimate pulmonary artery pressure.
- Right Heart Catheterization: Gold standard for confirming diagnosis and measuring pulmonary artery pressures.
- Imaging: Chest X-rays, CT scans, and MRI to visualize lung and heart structures and identify underlying causes.
- Other Tests: Pulmonary function tests, sleep studies, and blood tests to assess for associated conditions.

MANAGEMENT

The management of pulmonary hypertension involves addressing the underlying cause, improving symptoms, and slowing disease progression.

Medications

- Endothelin Receptor Antagonists (ERAs): Reduce vasoconstriction and improve blood flow.
- Phosphodiesterase-5 Inhibitors (PDE-5i): Increase nitric oxide availability, leading to vasodilation.
- Prostacyclin Analogues and Receptor Agonists: Promote vasodilation and inhibit platelet aggregation.

- Soluble Guanylate Cyclase (sGC) Stimulators: Enhance nitric oxide signaling and improve vascular function.
- Anticoagulants: Used in CTEPH to prevent further clot formation.

Non-Pharmacological Treatments

- Oxygen Therapy: For patients with hypoxemia to improve oxygenation.
- Exercise and Rehabilitation: Supervised exercise programs to improve physical conditioning and quality of life.
- Surgical Interventions: For selected patients, such as pulmonary thromboendarterectomy for CTEPH and lung transplantation in severe cases.

PROGNOSIS

The prognosis of pulmonary hypertension varies widely depending on the underlying cause and the severity at diagnosis. Early detection and appropriate management are crucial for improving outcomes.

FUTURE DIRECTIONS

Research in pulmonary hypertension is focused on understanding the molecular mechanisms of the disease, developing new treatments, and improving diagnostic techniques.

- Molecular Research: Studying the pathways involved in vascular remodeling and right heart dysfunction.
- New Therapies: Investigating novel drugs and combination therapies to target different pathways in pulmonary hypertension.
- Improved Diagnostics: Developing non-invasive methods for early detection and monitoring of disease progression.

DISCUSSION QUESTIONS

- What are the challenges in diagnosing pulmonary hypertension in its early stages?

- How do different treatment modalities (medication, surgery, lifestyle changes) complement each other in managing pulmonary hypertension?

CONCLUSION

Respiratory diseases and disorders represent a significant burden on global health, affecting millions of individuals and posing substantial challenges to healthcare providers. This comprehensive course, "Mastering Respiratory Diseases and Disorders: A Comprehensive Guide for Healthcare Providers," aims to equip healthcare professionals with the knowledge and skills necessary to diagnose, treat, and manage these conditions effectively.

Each chapter delves into the intricacies of respiratory health, from understanding the pathophysiology of common respiratory diseases such as asthma, COPD, pneumonia, and lung cancer to recognizing the impact of occupational and allergic respiratory diseases. Through detailed exploration of diagnostic tools, treatment strategies, and management practices, healthcare providers can enhance their clinical understanding and improve patient outcomes.

The course also emphasizes the importance of preventative measures, such as vaccinations, smoking cessation, and workplace safety, to reduce the incidence and severity of respiratory diseases. Furthermore, by addressing respiratory disorders in special populations like the elderly and those with occupational exposures, the course ensures a holistic approach to respiratory healthcare.

Mastering the complexities of respiratory diseases and disorders is crucial for healthcare providers dedicated to improving respiratory health. Through this course, healthcare providers can make informed decisions, deliver high-quality care, and ultimately enhance the quality of life for patients suffering from respiratory diseases.

REFERENCES

Barnes, P. J. (2010). *"New treatments for COPD."* Nature Reviews Drug Discovery

Bergeron, C., & Tulic, M. K. (2014*). "Asthma: From bronchodilators to immunomodulators."* Clinical Chest Medicine

Blanco, I., & Pérez de Llano, L. (2019*). "Chronic obstructive pulmonary disease and lung cancer: the missing link."* The Lancet Respiratory Medicine

Chan-Yeung, M., & Malo, J. L. (1995). *"Occupational asthma."* New England Journal of Medicine

Chung, K. F., & Adcock, I. M. (2008*). "Inflammatory mechanisms of asthma and COPD: Similarities and differences."* Immunology and Allergy Clinics of North America.

Decramer, M., Janssens, W., & Miravitlles, M. (2012). *"Chronic obstructive pulmonary disease."* The Lancet

Fishman, J. A. (2013). *"Pneumonia in the immunocompromised host."* The American Journal of Respiratory and Critical Care Medicine

Galiè, N., Humbert, M., Vachiery, J. L., Gibbs, S., Lang, I., Torbicki, A., ... & Hoeper, M. M. (2016). *"2015 ESC/ERS Guidelines for the diagnosis and treatment of pulmonary hypertension."* European Heart Journal